One Amazing Night

by Beverly J. Porter

illustrated by Jan Bower

Copyright © 2018 by Beverly J. Porter. All rights reserved. Illustrations © 2018 by Jan Bower. All rights reserved.

Published in the United States by Credo House Publishers, a division of Credo Communications, LLC, Grand Rapids, Michigan
www.credohousepublishers.com

Scriptures taken from the Holy Bible, New International Version®, NIV®. Copyright © 1973, 1978, 1984, 2011 by Biblica, Inc.™ Used by permission of Zondervan. All rights reserved worldwide. www.zondervan.com The "NIV" and "New International Version" are trademarks registered in the United States Patent and Trademark Office by Biblica, Inc.™

Edited and designed by Gary Bower.

ISBN 978-1-62586-143-6

Printed in the United States of America.

*Dedicated to my family,
especially Ethan, Jenny, Jolee, and Sophia*

One night long ago something amazing happened to me that I will never forget. It took place my first time guarding the sheep all night long with Abba[1] and Dod[2].

---

[1] *Abba* is Hebrew for Father.
[2] *Dod* is Hebrew for Uncle.

Abba had told me many times that I was too small and too young, but I had grown both taller and stronger. I had done my chores faithfully for Ima[3] every day, hoping to one day work with the sheep. Abba finally agreed that I was ready, and I was determined not to disappoint him.

---

[3] *Ima* is Hebrew for Mother.

It had been a long day of hard work. We had to watch the sheep closely, keep them together so that none would be lost, and at the same time watch for any wolf, bear, or thief that could harm the sheep. It could be dangerous for the shepherd as well as the sheep.

"A good shepherd must always be alert and ready," Abba reminded me.

All day long the sheep grazed among the tender, green, meadow grasses and drank cool water from the stream.

Later, we led them to the fold for the night. Daylight dimmed into darkness, and the air grew colder as I helped Dod gather sticks for the evening fire.

Abba built the fire. We warmed ourselves beside it as we ate thick-crusted bread, some goat cheese that Ima had packed for us, and then roasted apples over the fire. The thought of that still makes my mouth water — the apples tasted so juicy and sweet. We had plenty, so I ate until I was full!

By that time, it had grown very dark. White stars sparkled bright against the black sky. In the distance, we saw a faint glow rising from distant campfires near the town of Bethlehem.

Dod and Abba talked about things they had heard, and said that the town was crowded with visitors who had come for a census.

"What's a census?" I asked.

"It's a counting of the people," Abba explained. "Caesar Augustus ordered it for the whole Roman Empire, so all men must visit the town of their ancestry."

Soon the crackle of the fire and gentle bleating of the sheep were the only sounds. I felt very sleepy as I rubbed my eyes and yawned.

"Time to sleep," said Abba. "Dod will stay awake and guard the sheep awhile, then we'll take our turn."

Suddenly, a bright flash lit the sky above like brilliant sunlight. We all jumped to our feet, but I stood behind Abba and shook with fear. Then a beautiful, glowing, angel appeared! The angel smiled at us and spoke with a kind voice:

"Do not be afraid. I bring you good news that will cause great joy for all the people. Today in the town of David a Savior has been born to you; He is the Messiah, the Lord. This will be a sign to you: You will find a baby wrapped in cloths and lying in a manger."[4]

I trembled and thought I would faint when more angels appeared. There were so many that they nearly filled the sky! They all began to praise God in the most wonderful voices I had ever heard, and my fear simply melted away. They said:

"Glory to God in the highest heaven, and on earth peace to those on whom His favor rests." [5]

We stood watching and listening when they suddenly left. The sky became dark and silent once more.

---

[4] Luke 2:10-12
[5] Luke 2:14

It seemed like a dream! We all began talking at once about the angels. Finally, Abba said, "Let's go to Bethlehem and see this thing that has happened…"[6]

"I will stay and watch the sheep," Dod said. "You two go."

Abba and I nearly ran the whole way to Bethlehem.

But something puzzled me and I asked Abba, "Why would the baby Savior be in a manger?"

Abba replied, "It must be all they could find for a bed. He must have been born to someone without a home there. Perhaps to someone visiting Bethlehem for the census."

---

[6] Luke 2:15

When we finally reached Bethlehem, the town seemed noisy. People talked and some animals moved about as we made our way through the crowded streets.

We asked around to see if anyone knew about a visiting woman who would soon give birth. Some men pointed us toward an inn.

Abba spoke to the innkeeper, who said, "Yes, a man asked for a room, but I had none to offer him. He told me his wife was about to have a baby, so I offered the use of my stable. It was the best I could do."

"Would you show us, please?" Abba asked.

The innkeeper led us to the stable and knocked gently at the door.

"Joseph, someone is here to see you."

The wooden door creaked open slightly, revealing a tall man.

"Can I help you?"

"We've been sent by…um…messengers," Abba explained. "We were told that we would find a baby… the Savior."

The man lifted a lantern and looked closely at our faces for a moment. Then he smiled and welcomed us inside.

"We have visitors, Mary," he said softly.

In a corner of the quiet stable a young woman rested. She looked tired, but happy. Beside her stood a manger — an animal feeding trough. Inside the manger, lying on a fresh bed of straw, was a baby, just as the angel had said.

Slowly, quietly, I stepped closer to get a better look. The baby looked so tiny. He was wrapped tightly in cloths and his little eyes were closed.

I felt such a sense of peace and joy! Even the animals inside the stable were calm as Abba and I knelt on the stable floor.

The ima sat beside the manger, gently stroking her baby's cheek. She listened silently to every word as we told her what we had seen and heard. Her eyes were kind and she had a gentle smile.

I wanted to stay, but Abba said that we must be on our way. We had to tell others about the birth of Christ the Lord.

Joseph and Mary nodded and smiled. We knew they understood.

As Abba closed the stable door behind us, I exclaimed, "I can hardly wait to tell Dod and Ima!"

"Yes," agreed Abba, "This is good news — for all people. Our long awaited Savior has come!"

Many years have passed, and I am much older now. I have guarded the sheep over many dark and quiet nights. But I will never forget my very first night watching the sheep with Abba and Dod. The night when we saw and heard angels! The night when we found a baby in a manger — the baby who was Christ the Lord, our Savior!

That was one amazing night!

*This story is based on Luke 2:1-20. My late father-in-law Darcy
read Luke 2 aloud each Christmas Eve as the entire family gathered around.
We continue this tradition in our family and our son Darcy now reads the text,
often from his grandfather's Bible.*

About the Author

Beverly J. Porter writes from her farmhouse office in the countryside near Rockford, Michigan. She and her husband Ron have raised three sons, and the family now includes two daughters-in-law, six grandchildren, and one great-grandchild. The author of numerous articles in various genres, her first book, "Hills, Deals, and Stills," a memoir, was published in 2015. "One Amazing Night" is her first children's book.

About the Illustrator

Jan Bower has won numerous awards for her oil portraits and picture books. "One Amazing Night" is her sixteenth children's book. She and her husband Gary work in their country studios near Traverse City, Michigan. Their twelve children and twenty-four grandchildren drop by frequently. When Jan is not at her easel, there is a good chance she is gardening or canning. **www.janbower.com**

Thank You...

*to talented artist Jan Bower, who, through countless hours,
created the beautiful illustrations for this book,
and to Gary Bower, who so graciously and wisely edited this story.
It has been an honor to work with you.*
– Beverly J. Porter